I0756276

FINISHING LINE PRESS
www.finishinglinepress.com

Lacquer is a Thrilling Word

Poems and Short Prose
By

Barrie Cole

Finishing Line Press
Georgetown, Kentucky

Lacquer is a Thrilling Word

For Ruben and Sita

ISBN 979-8-89990-469-1 First Edition

Acknowledgments

I knew the Other Ways it Could Be appeared in *Airplane Reading*
Haiku and *Message* appeared as monologues in *Reverse Gossip* directed by Jen Moniz.
Down the Hill appeared as a monologue in *Reality as an Activity* and was produced by Theatre Oobleck.
To Do was originally commissioned by KellyAnn Corcoran for T*en to One*
On Poetry originally appeared as part of Ian Belknap's *Write Club* at the Poetry Foundation

Also: a thousand columns and rows of thanks to my friends, family, Avi, my partner, my dear friend Julie for decades of encouragement, belief, and collaboration, also reviewers, actors, readers, audiences, editors, assistants, designers, fellow writers, mentors, teachers and communities.

Publisher: Leah Huete de Maines
Editor: Christen Kincaid
Cover Art: Kate Roth, *Landscape number 2*
Author Photo: Jeffrey Bivens
Cover Design: Elizabeth Maines McCleavy

Order online: www.finishinglinepress.com
also available on amazon.com

Author inquiries and mail orders:
Finishing Line Press
PO Box 1626
Georgetown, Kentucky 40324
USA

Contents

"The vowels in the wood are cared for by birds who cover them in strawberry leaves."

—Mary Ruefle

"In came in there, came in there come out of there. In came in come out of there. Come out there in came in there. Come out of there and come out of there of there and in and come out of there."

—Gertrude Stein

1

Save the Date

This is an invitation to do what
you were going to do anyway.

You are cordially invited to have the day
you were already planning on having,
the difference being that now,
you have been officially invited.

So congratulations on being selected!

If you like, you can imagine an envelope with your name on it
handwritten in calligraphy, bearing a special edition
postage stamp with illustrations of rare corals and mollusks.

No need to RSVP.

Closer

A sailboat barely moves
beneath an audience of pink-toothed clouds.

No swimmers or lifeguards yet,
only lifeguard chairs made taller with green flags.

Camouflage to merge with anything.
I've seen grackles mix themselves into tree trunks.

Today I'm sizzle. I sputter.
I pepper with hiss.

I emptied a basket of unmatched socks
down the staircase. They swam like fish down a waterfall.

My grandma had a staircase of elegant chins leading up to her face.
She could perform headstands underwater.

I had a venus flytrap on my windowsill and a
sister with a canopy bed who stuck a thumbtack up her nose.

Mark Doty writes, "Heaven steadies and concentrates near the lavender."
I want to steady and concentrate too. I want to be like heaven.

So put me near the lavender or
at least bring me some lavender soap.

Let's gather up some tiny hotel shampoos and lather
a lucky recipient's head.

Accordion buses play themselves.
Being in one is as good as being inside a whale.

But the knife-sharpener doesn't come to the farmer's market anymore.
I miss the scrape sound on the stone. It rearranged my depression.

So fine, it's decided: I'm going to give you a
guitar filled with cherries.
They will ripen as you strum.

The Breakup

Before you began saying those sentences made from
barbed wire & shit, before the talk we tried to have
that was more like an interrogation than a conversation,
before we were interrupted by the car alarm blaring out
like a relentless ache matching some unsounded sound in
us, a frozen gulp, before the starkest sentence too,
so stark it was skeletal, no fat on it whatsoever, before we
arrived in the middle of the nastiest paragraph within
which we flung rocks & bricks of words, before the
trip had even begun, the trip meant to rekindle, but which
refused to spark, before we went to that garbage beach
in Florida where you told me you'd cheated & I couldn't
stop seeing you do it, while you insisted it didn't matter,
that it was nothing, no thing, no thing at all, & the smelly
water, red tide, dead fish in criss-cross patterns, globs of
jellyfish, thick ropes of seaweed studded with broken glass,
a man sucking a cigar while his leathery daughters
sprawled across towels, greased-up, talking about booze:
We'll get so fucked-up. And the anorexic woman by
the shoreline, with legs like drinking straws speed-walking
back & forth while her partner jogged beside her, thrusting
a granola bar to her mouth, begging her eat: *Stop this,*
stop this, stop, please. Before we entered the car, arrived
at the airport, took our seats on the plane, before you slammed
the shade shut, rejecting a sky, before the plane thudded
down, before we went through what felt like 1,316 revolving
doors revolving & revolving like pottery wheels caked with
crud, carousels with monsters instead of horses, fans made from
knives, before we scaled that dumb, too high bed, before we fell
asleep at last facing away from each other's faces. Before you
faced a wall & I faced a door, away & away, before all that.

Object Relations

Sometimes I think about the objects I possess; I think about their ancestry. I think about how they have descended from thrift stores or other stores, or from other people, or other places. I think about their collaborations; the pencil with the sharpener, the couch with the dust, the teacup with the teabag.

Sometimes friends visit from out of town and we visit museums and look at objects both inside and outside of glass cases. Our relationships with these objects could be known as our object relations.

At the Thorne miniature room at the Art Institute of Chicago there are many, many very tiny objects inside many, many tiny rooms. There are rugs the size of a child's palm and grandfather clocks no bigger than a book of matches and a book of matches no bigger than a ladybug. It's a lot to take in.

It is also true that sometimes I see a young woman do her important work in the cafe section of the supermarket near my home. I go there to write sometimes and also have a salad. I assemble the salad from the salad bar before I eat it, but that is hardly the point.

The point is that the young woman's work involves clearing objects from tables and then wiping the tables with a grey rag and then clearing them and wiping the same tables again. She is so careful, so exact.

Sometimes I find watching her mesmerizing and I am filled with something that is either awe or something so close to awe that it might as well be awe, although I find myself a little embarrassed to use a word like *awe* because it is such a grand word.

Sometimes I think about getting a therapist and then cheating on that therapist with a different therapist. I imagine letting this therapeutic infidelity go on for a while, months perhaps; seeing two therapists, comparing their styles; each of their various similar or dissimilar takes on my problems. I imagine confessing to each of them about the other, but only at the point when I could no longer tolerate my own duplicity. Maybe the therapists would care about my cheating and maybe they wouldn't. Maybe the caring would stay in me and it would be mine to contend with and the therapists would hardly think of it or me at all.

Sometimes I wonder why so many of my closest friends are alcoholics; the kind of alcoholics who no longer drink and practice steps that are not dance steps, but are a bit like dance steps all the same. These friends go to meetings where sometimes people smoke cigarettes on the other kind of steps outside which are made of cement and go up, up, up, to a door, and down, down, down, to the sidewalk. There is a rusty metal railing too which gets cold to the touch in winter.

And maybe someone is asking another someone to the sober holiday party: kids welcome, $25 tickets before Thanksgiving, $30 after, and $40 at the door.

Sometimes I wonder if there could be a single person who wasn't some kind of addict. Sometimes I congratulate myself again for quitting smoking, even though I haven't had a cigarette in many years.

Sometimes I wrestle with sentences even though sentences and I are in completely different weight classes. (I am heavier.) Sometimes I can pin down a verb like a real pro and the crowd of me goes wild. Often, I lose and losing, well, losing is what it is.

Sometimes I like to list several foods all in a row. It is best to do this with foods containing carbohydrates. One example of such a list is: pasta, cake, bread, eclair, muffin, bun, biscuit, doughnut. Participating in this particular activity is comforting. It's like counting sheep or trucks or all the days until something terrible is over like a temporary work position in an office with melancholy cubicles and a 20-minute lunch break.

Sometimes I think about syntax and what the tax is for and how in the world I could ever pay it. Could anyone ever pay all of their syntax?

Sometimes I want to pull all the numbers out of the dispenser at the deli counter and throw them up in the air like confetti. And when they float down, it would be like I was in a grocery store-themed snowglobe.

Sometimes I want to give a stranger an extravagant gift like a gold watch or a mirror in a lacquered frame or a large, chocolate bunny made from solid chocolate through and through. Sometimes I think about just how sad hollow chocolate rabbits really are. So much emptiness.

Sometimes I think about what constitutes a gift and I think, under the right circumstances, any object or non-object could count as one.

Sometimes I wonder if a poem counts as an object or not.
Sometimes I wonder if a kiss counts as an object or not too.

Sometimes I imagine picking up poems and kisses and putting them down and picking them up and putting them down again and again like the young woman, Natalie, her name is Natalie, I just remembered. Natilie with the grey rag, and delicate wrists, who works at the cafe inside the grocery store.

New Fortune Cookie Fortunes

There are babies in your future, all of them wonderfully fat and wearing green sweaters with matching hats. If you happen to have a lack of fondness for babies, don't worry, these particular babies will be the exceptions.

Someone will give you a lamination machine as a gift. You will laminate a small black comb, a dirty shoelace, and a portrait of your cousin you've scribbled in blue-green magic marker on an index card you'd been using, up until then, as a bookmark.

On Wednesdays, in September, you will experience moments of bonafide joy, mostly because all the words you love for no good reason will be spoken to you throughout the day; *haphazard, antelope, comma, lacquer, perambulate, stanza.* It will be as if some kind of word fairy has your whole back-a true friend.

You will find a small clay figure of a woman or a snail on the sidewalk near the library. It is yours to keep or give away. I'm pretty sure you'll give it to Pam, but I wouldn't bet on it.

Your lucky letters are every letter: A to Z. Each one is for you. If you run out of letters and need more luck, just combine letters or switch to numbers.

You will receive awards for going to work, for going to the dentist, for putting on socks, for voting in smaller, local elections, and showering. If you take a bath, you'll receive an award. as well as an additional trophy in the shape of a bathtub.

The Adult

My daughter is on a plane to
New Orleans.
She's turning 21 tomorrow.
She's with Angel, her friend with
long, black hair. Angel
is a twin. My son's girlfriend
Sadie has curly hair
She is a twin too.

Yes, doubleness is bubbling up
skipping its stone across my life.
But there is only one
of my daughter who
as an infant would knock
on my breast with a fist
while she sucked.

When I don't hear from her by the time
the plane is scheduled to land, I take off
the "p" in plane and imagine
her walking down a lane instead-
a charming cul- de- sac
lined with cell phones,
a park at the bulb, and moss
with a give on the ground.

Micro Poems

They are so small you will
need a magnifying glass just to read them
Some require a microscope
They are the size of dust specks
and snowflakes
Some are only one letter long
usually a vowel
Others have a comma after nothing
a line break after no line

To Do

First, I have to go there to get that thing and while I'm there, I'm going to go somewhere near that place to get that other thing and I have to sign a paper, too. I need to pick up that other stuff and get that other thing and those other things are waiting for me too and I don't want to be late and I didn't finish what I was supposed to finish so I'll make some calls or I'll try to stop somehow, somewhere and finish and maybe I can eat something while I do that or not eat.

I have the ankle appointment too and I have to go to the bank too and I have to drop the kids off too and I have to get the dog the shots and bring her back afterwards. I have to remember too about that other, other thing too, and that other, other, other thing too.

I need to mail that gift. I need to buy stamps. I need to go shopping because I have nothing to wear or eat and the kids need all those supplies for school. They will want to get the supplies themselves because there are colors to consider and styles beyond colors, so I think we will do all that after everything else.

I forgot about the appointment which means I'll have to call and apologize and reschedule. I will have to remember to do all of this in my head because I will be driving and so I will not be able to write any of it down.

I will have to take online traffic school because last week I was not using the bluetooth with the cell phone. I didn't even have it on speaker and when I was pulled over, the cop said, "Where do you think you are, your living room?" I didn't answer. Why would I?

I will need to stop at some point to meditate near a tree. I will need to finish reading the book for the discussion. Oh please, just who do I think I'm kidding? I will need to begin the book and get at least half way through the first chapter and remember to bring some wine. Do I have wine? Do I need to buy wine?

I will need to arrange everything with the kids and their father for next week. I can do that by email, or by phone, or in person, or through texting, or perhaps even through telepathy. It's not completely out of the realm of possibility, is it? I will think about whether it is or is not out of the realm of possibility.

I will need to figure out dating. I will need to figure out sex. I will need to figure out my entire life. I will need a plan. I can use some of the time driving to plan. I will need some post-it notes.

I will get post-it notes when I take the kids for school supplies. I will need to buy flowers. I will need some sunlight for vitamin D. I will need some supplementary vitamins, as well as other methods of fortification. I will need to get cleaning supplies in order to clean. I will need to clean. I will need to get gas and a car wash. I will need to get some coffee or a soft-serve cone.

I will need to think about stress. I will need to think about injustice, climate change, rising facism, poverty, war, and so much more. I will need to think about and employ various coping mechanisms. I will need to search for change and also a snack for the person with matted hair and a ripped, yellow raincoat in the center lane. The rip is on his sleeve and so when he moves his arm, the rip moves too, like an underling sweeping across the matching yellow lines.

I will need to notice the surprise doe and baby fawn right off the highway. I will need to call someone about seeing the surprise doe and baby fawn off the highway and talk about what it could mean that I have seen this and talk about Carl Jung. I will need to write down my dreams in a special journal made from recycled dust. I will get the journal during the school supplies errand. I need to be one of those people who is intensely alive.

I forgot to get the flowers. I will get hydrangeas. If they don't have hydrangeas, I will get tulips or roses. I will bloom myself. I will get glue-sticks and scissors too. I will get those items apart from the school supplies errand or maybe within it. I will go to the dollar store and buy ten things I might need someday including all the things the kids might need or forget to buy when we go to buy school supplies.

I will give myself a breast exam in the car. I will listen to the French vocabulary podcast. I will make up dazzling limericks that are not meant to be funny and won't be. I will cry about so many things and then I will pull myself together with a magic drawstring.

And later, after picking up the kids, I will listen to them tell stories from their last day of camp. I will go back to camp five minutes later to retrieve the bathing suit which someone has hung on the metal bike rack. The suit is blue and wet and dripping drop by drop onto the sidewalk having its own little sun shower while leaving a quarter-sized puddle on the ground.

I will pick up dinner. I will pick myself up. I will pick up everything. I will drop everything off. I will walk the dog. I will feed the rabbit. I will notice the rhythm of my breath. I will eat a Tic-Tac. I will do everything. I will make promises to my children. I will promise them everything. I will mean everything I say. I will be an extraordinary twenty-first century human being. I will be organic. I will make the world better. I will be cutting edge. I will be available. I will surrender.

Haiku

Hi, I'm on the train.
Will you help me write a Haiku?

So far, I have:
I am on the train.

Yes, yes, a nature theme is traditional.
We can write a traditional haiku, a non-traditional
haiku, or a combination of both.

What?
Oh, that's good.
Say it again: *It moves just like a river.*
Yes, that's good.

I can't think of how to end it though.
I am going home.
What do you think?

I am on the train.
It moves just like a river.
I am going home.

How about, *I'm on my way home?*
Maybe it should be: *It moves just like the river?*
Do you think that sounds better?
Should it feel faster?

How about:

I ride this train line
It's a rushing river
carrying us home

Never mind, on the *home.*
It doesn't sound right.
How about

I am on the train.
The train is like a river.
I will be home soon.

Shit, this Haiku
sounds like a text message.
It's awful. It sounds like:

On the train,
Be home soon.
I picked up the pizza.

Your line is the only good line,
the middle line,
the one about the river.

Drive Thru

I'll have the breakfast sandwich please.
I'll have an iced coffee too, heavy on the ice.
I'll have the sunrise with its pink, gold, and red ribbons of varying thicknesses, please.
I'll have the blurry areas too, where everything smudges together.
I'll have the sunlight darting out in glinting points.
I'll have the dawn chorus, the full-length version, live.
I'll have all the chirping, all the calling, all the singing, at the highest volume with the brightest setting.
Give it to me.

I Swear, I Did Not Intend

to eat the ripe plum from your tree
My arm was pulled by a muscular longing

I only had to part the heavy air to find
one brightening at the bottom for my hand to cup

By the time you caught me, my mouth was
oozing wet gold

I made things worse when I began to recite the poem
What the hell is an icebox? You asked

Nevermind, I said. *Sorry again*, I said
But I wasn't sorry

Walking home, I felt the pit slip quietly
into the dark clutch of my cheek

Instruments

A chance at satisfaction must include
easy to locate pens.
Pens have to be everywhere, all around
within arm's reach or
even closer.

Here's what I do:

Every five years or so,
I order 1,000 pens on Ebay.

1,000 pens is a scribbling army,
a ballpoint mob.

The box is heavier than you might think.
44 pounds. (I weighed it.)

It arrives with a genuine *thump*.

These pens from the bay are mostly
misprints with smudged letters, incorrect
telephone numbers, all types of mistakes.

And so, I find myself writing with a pen from
an auto body shop in Nebraska or a
real estate office in Missouri only
the "r" in real estate is missing and
reads *eal estate*.

I think of eels.

Sawtooth, Spiny, Snowflake, Cutthroat, Electric

I imagine an estate filled with them.

They loop around pergolas and arches.
They arrange themselves on bannisters.
They hold races in the reflecting pool.

They place themselves on top of fountain spouts
to experience brief moments of elevation.

Sometimes, they gather into a circle, head to tail,
tail to head, and then, for fun, they spin.

And later, when the pencil of day is erased,
when the great pen of the world
releases the ink of night
from its narrow, plastic tube
the electric eels power up with a buzz
and illuminate the property.

Still

I tell myself I am still a good person if I broke my glasses accidentally because I left them on the floor and stepped on them and I am still a good person if I lost my glasses entirely and now can hardly see and I am still a good person if I couldn't remember exactly where I parked my car and also which direction is east, west, north, or south and I am still a good person if I have had an unfortunate haircut, the kind where there are bangs of insanity, the kind wherein cutting more could not even begin to improve it, a haircut that makes purchasing a wig a genuine consideration and I am still a good person if I paid the bill late and I was too anxious to attend the party and too anxious to say hello to the neighbor and so pretended not to see her at all and this was no surprise because I do this more than I do not, but I am still good. Probably.

And I think that if I keep making mistakes, maybe one day, I'll just stay very still because if I don't move at all, I won't make any mistakes, but I still won't be dead. I'll be a still life of myself. I'll place myself into a position in which I'll resemble some kind of vessel-a vase or a bowl. I'll climb onto a small table, near a window with a heavy, velvet curtain. I'll surround myself with nectarines and apples, a tight bunch of lavender, a sprig of this, a sprig of that as well as hawk, bluejay, and wild turkey feathers. A sleeping fox that will look dead for effect only will politely arrange its rusty tail in such a way that it dangles over the table's edge creating the illusion of a furry path to the cornucopia. A few crumpled white linen napkins with embroidered borders will cast shadows on the walls. I'll try to convince myself again and again that a still life is still a life.

Important Information

I've made you these windchimes from whole, ripe mangoes.
When it's windy, you can listen to their quiet, thumpy song.

Later, we can pretend to be farmers. We'll grow crops of blank space.
After our workdays, we'll rest in meadows of emptiness between
parentheses.

I want you to know that the reason I deposited squash blossoms in all the
postal boxes is because they've been living on diets of paper.

Also, consider conveyor belts at grocery stores.
They speak in poems and come with their own plastic linebreak tools.

I love their black, rubbery paper scrolls. Last Wednesday, ahead of me,
in the ten items or less line, I watched a poem being conveyed:

Lettuce, dishsoap, mushrooms, lemons, ballpoint pens, cottage cheese,
maple syrup in a tiny metal house, flame-drenched, marble-sized
tomatoes piled up inside a see-thru chest.

I Know What Happens When We Die.

First, we are stripped down in layers
by light.

Yes it's bright, but it's no biggie,
we're dead.

The light is a strip-poker champion.
She wins and wins.

The clothes pile up into a great heap known as the
Coatbed of All Coatbeds.

Under our clothes, we're not naked.
We're still us, only now, as air.

We breeze into an echoey stadium
where piñatas filled with magnolias and lilies
spill and spill. Badges are delivered
bearing our new names followed by a
mandatory meet and greet.

Guess what?
Our new names are words we loved in life!

We float about whispering: *Nice to meet you, Juxtaposition.*
Likewise, Marsupial Reflect. I'm Conundrum. Have you met Collide
Tomorrow?

And then slowly, like a sunset
a territory opens up. We walk into it.
It walks into us. And then, like kids
after school, we shout, *I'm home*
into the forever.

Suggestion Box

I suggest we lavish butter upon crackers and scones and then perhaps spread butter upon some walls. We can pretend the walls are toast. We can use the butter knives located in the employee kitchen for this activity. Josh won't mind.

I suggest we take a comb and gently comb the hair of a child and then the hair of a monster and then the hair of an elderly person and then the hair of someone without hair. We can coo over the loveliness of the imaginary hair on the head of the bald person in particular as we comb it and say sweet things about the texture, ringlets, locks, and such. We can say things like:

What silky locks you have. What a substantial braid. Your curls remind me of multiple spiral staircases up to a roof garden—a garden with a shady spot and probably a fountain too—solar-powered.

I suggest we learn where our appendixes are or were exactly and then write appendixes about our findings. And then, working backward, we'll write accompanying books.

Names of Boats

If someone gave you a boat and they said here is your boat and now it is your boat and you should name your boat because boats have names and yes, yes, it is true, all boats have names

and

some people name their cars or bicycles or even their roller-skates and sometimes when they name their roller skates, they even choose two names (one for each skate) like Harold and Maude, Benny and The Jets, or Bagel and Creamcheese

but

it is not required to name your skates, car, bicycle, scooter, or motorcycle, but a boat must be named for reasons unknown and, yes, it must be named and in that particular way a boat is like a baby, and a boat is also similar to a baby because both the word *boat* and the word *baby* begin with the letter "b" and both must be named.

but

if you have a boat and a baby it is probably unwise to name both of them the same name because if you did do this, you'd discover that when speaking of your boat or of your baby there would be a need to specify which one you were speaking of

and

if you were speaking of them both, you'd have to say the name twice and that could get terribly redundant and then when people spoke of you they would describe you as a redundant person, a redundant person who had a boat and a baby with the same name

so

you might consider naming your baby one name and naming your boat another name and I think Silky would be a good name for a boat and Otis would be a good name for a baby or

you could, of course, go the other way around, and call a baby Silky and a boat Otis
or just do what you want, because what do I know?

I have no boat and my babies grew up.

The Summary

This summary has nothing to do with summer and everything to do with math and by math I mean addition and by addition I mean adding up.

I don't mean an addition as in an extra room, floor, or section added on to an existing structure as in, "Hey, you should come over and see our new addition. We've added an elevator. We've added a solarium. We've added a deck."

Furthermore, by addition, I don't mean adding a human to a family. New humans are great, but that is not what I am talking about here, just so we're clear.

So, what will I be adding in this summary? What will I be summarizing and what are the pluses and the no minuses?

Well, I will begin with lattes because coffee is necessary and of the available ways to consume it, if lattes are options, why not have one or more than one? So: Latte plus latte plus latte plus latte equals four lattes in all, plus ten good palm trees, plus a Mary Oliver poem in which she goes on for some lines within a stanza about the terrible beak of a bird. She's looking into it, inside the poem, Mary Oliver or the speaker, which in this case, I believe is Mary Oliver is gazing into the beak itself and she's describing it as the most terrible cup she will ever enter. But why? Why is the beak of a bird a terrible cup?

I suppose the beak-cup is our prehistorically programmed human hunger, or life itself or death itself or both life and death themselves. She's talking about the beak as a frightening portal, a tunnel-cup of existence rubbing against non-existence. I'm adding it into the summary.

So latte plus latte plus latte plus latte plus palm trees plus Mary Oliver's treatment of the beak in her poem with brief commentary, plus my entire dream life including the dreams in which I am fishing with a pen as a fishing pole and all the rest of the dreams too including the dream shards.

This is a complicated or a convoluted summary or perhaps both, and perhaps I should apologize and maybe I will. I could add it in; add an apology into the summary, but first I will add in helium, some tanks of helium, as many as are necessary for a lift-up and a voice-change too in case there are kids who want to do that kind of thing because they like to do that, most kids do like to, they do.

And also, enough helium to fill so, so, so many balloons, as many as possible or are necessary. There will obviously be many, many colors available, not of helium, which is of course, colorless, but of balloons. Some of them will have a special sheen, a special luster, an opalescence if you will.

A side note: I purchased 50 golden balloons for my parent's 50th golden wedding anniversary and having ordered such a thing, and then having the bundle of them arrive like a floating collection of gigantic pendants, really did it for me.

Also, Lisa, from the balloon company referred to the group of balloons as a bouquet. Having had this experience, I would order a bouquet of balloons again with or without occasion or reason.

Another side note: The word helium probably ends with an um because it is not sure whether it will end up inside of a balloon or not.

So to review: There are balloons and lattes, palm trees, a substantial beak metaphor courtesy of the late Mary Oliver plus lacquer because lacquer is such a good word with the c and q next to each other in such sexiness and splendor. Oh yes, *lacquer* is a thrilling word indeed. Why we could pour the lacquer all over, all over, all over:

We could pour lacquer over the balloons, over Mary Oliver's terrible beak-cup, the palm trees, We could pour the lacquer over everything except the lattes. We will leave the lattes as they are. We will leave them lacquerless, without lacquer.

Next, Billy Collins, the poet: We will not add him in, but we will add the town wherein he resides at present, a town called Winter Park, Florida, and the name of the town of course is so funny as I am certain there is no snow or much of anything resembling what most think of as winter in Winter Park, Florida. The entire situation is so much like one of his poems.

Oh, the irony!

Furthermore, what is especially good about adding Winter Park, Florida, to the summary is that everything else we have already added or will add afterwards can fit inside Winter Park, Florida. Winter Park, Florida can be the holding place. There is poetry there already. Even its name has poetry in it, so why not? Let us add to Winter Park, the terrible beak cup in the Mary Oliver poem.

Let us add the palm trees of which Florida is quite filled with as it is, the lattes, the helium inside of and also outside of the balloons, the lacquer and the c and q side by side celebration within that ornate word. And while we are at it, let us add in massages, hibiscus, ruffles, and hexagons. Let us add in spoons and zithers too.

I am the transmitter and this is the transmission.

Let us add in many dogs. We will have a catalog of dogs, a log of dogs so we can keep track of them all. Quite a few will be small dogs for reasons of space. They too will be recorded in the dog log.

Also pools: Pools of light as well as swimming pools. Much like palm trees, Florida has an ample supply of swimming pools so they should be in the summary.

Pools should also be included in the summary for swimming. Swimming is the best way to experience oneself as a fish and also a real way to cool off in hot weather. Win, win.

What else? Towels, elephants, bagels, a small collection of ghosts.

I am the transmitter and this is the transmission. This is the summary. And summer will come again one day. Just wait, just wait for June. I promise, you'll see.

Message

Hi.

Can you be ready for something new?
Can you put yourself into a state of readiness?

I want to test something,
but first you have to be ready,
and in order to be ready,
you have to clear your mind.

I'll wait,
I'll wait until you're ready.

Wow, that was fast.
That's good.
I'm impressed.
It usually takes a lot
longer for me to get ready.

Okay, so, I want to see
if I can send you a text
with my mind.

I'm completely serious.
Why would I be joking?
I'm not joking.

Apparently, there's a 4th dimension.
It's holographic.

I want to enter the 4th dimension and once I'm there,
I'll send you a text to see if it works.

Okay, so I'm going to do it.
I'm going to send you a text with my mind.

It's only going to be one word, but if it works, I can move onto sentences and paragraphs and then, at some point, after some practice, I'll be able to text you something like an entire book.

It will be like a download, but without computers.

Ok, so, I'm going to count to three and then I'm going to send you the mind text.

1, 2. 3.

Okay, sent.
Did you get it?

Alright, I'll send it again.

Really be open to it; really be available to
receive it in the 4th dimension.

Okay, sent.

Flower?
Wow, so close!

Well, my word was necklace.
It's close, because there can be necklaces of flowers.
You know, like in Hawaii.
They're called leis. They're garlands,
garlands of flowers.

I do think it worked.
I think it worked a little.
I think it almost worked.

Out of Town

I have a passionate appreciation for your abundant eyebrows that caterpillar across your forehead. My review of them: so attractive, so furry, so beguiling, so great.

How about this? While I am away, take me grocery shopping with you on the phone. Tell me what you are picking out: A pomegranate, bananas, artichokes, a large bag of rice, oatmeal, a pack of sponges; yellow and soft on one side, green and rough on the other, sardines in olive oil, noodles in various shapes: wheel, spaghetti, and spiral.

The engine of summer is whirring.

I want to be in it with you.

I love you with gold and amber tree sap.

I love you with sections of ice floating in parallelograms on the lake

I want to give you a good day, an extravagant dessert, a ruffled outfit, a vaccination against depression, a small spool of happiness, and several sighs of relief.

I want to give you a new name like Hologram Shimmer Thrill or Sexy Cloud Parade along with a few good luck charms on a convenient keychain.

I want to describe you in public while standing on a crate or a stoop or a curb. I would describe you as a melon, an heirloom, an elaborate beach umbrella, a honeycomb psalm. I would describe you as welcome heat in winter whooshing out from a vent.

2

After the Meet & Greet

I dreamt I told people my name was Thyme, spelled with an H.
I dreamt I told people my name was Nighttime.
I dreamt I told people my name was Lake Michigan.
I dreamt I told people my name was Walden Pond.
I dreamt I told people my name was Various Bodies Of Water.
I dreamt I told people my name was Water.
Just Water.
No last name.

The State of Affairs

It's pretty bad, yes it's pretty bad, because for the most part it's terrible, a bummer, really bumming us out big time and things haven't been good for a really long time and because of that, well, we tried to go bowling as a sort of medicine, but even bowling was a bust because the bowling alley ran out of certain rental shoe sizes and so many of us had to wear shoes that were too big and so we had to walk like clowns, or the shoes were too small, pinching our toes mercilessly, even causing a few of us to hobble.

And, the available bowling balls did not have the weights and colors that we liked best and so we had to bowl with balls that had colors that were not to our liking such as a red, white, and blue ball that was far too patriotic for how we were feeling at the time.

And another ball had a purple color that I never want to see again on a bowling ball or on anything else for that matter because it was such a nauseating, headache inducing purple.

And other balls were attractive, both with marbled designs and shine, wax even, but those balls were so heavy, we could hardly lift them or take them off their racks and some were so light that they were more like cotton balls or marbles than the bowling balls they were masquerading as. They were all disguise, no blessing.

And, as I've already explained, we had to wear shoes that pinched our toes, or shoes that the heels of our feet lifted out from as if our feet were puppets. My God.

What I'm trying to get across is that those of us who had to wear rental shoes that were much, bigger than our feet, well, as we walked toward the bowling lanes to take our turns, to knock down the pins as is the object of the activity, what I'm saying is, that if our heels had had faces, they'd have looked like people drowning, yet trying so hard not to drown, struggling over and over to come up for air, to stay above water, to survive, with every, single step.

Sting

She tells me that while having lunch
a bee flew into her mouth and stung her tongue.

Her tongue swelled and gleamed
like a wet ruby, a glob of song.

A wasp flew out of my refrigerator once,
And people that should not have died
died anyway.
So, I too know about stun.

We can wear grief shawls over our bathing suits.
We can find a shoal to swim out to.
We can interlace our fingers and cry
into the expanse.

Even mussels are tear-shaped.
Their shells, water's black petals
With a soft-shoe foot inside
secreting threads like garlic from a press
for clinging to rock, to here.

They stay as long as they can
growing wiry sea beards.
Such winsome old men with
soft, coppery bodies.

Yesterday, I thought I saw a squid in my sink
with arms like banjos, but it was only the
measuring spoons on their wiry ring.

I miss all my dead friends, especially Bill,
who shot himself in the head under a pillow
to cloak the noise and splatter.

It was the drink that got him.
It was the beatings in childhood
that got the drink.

Liquor is nothing like the sea.
And neither, I suppose, are we.

Shimmy and Revolve

I want to buy 2 bones.
One for my dog and
one for myself.

I'll lie on the floor with
her and we'll grunt as we attack them
tearing off the meat and fat.
We'll bite like a fight.

We'll suck out the marrow and let it
combine with our drool.
We'll slurp and hum.

We'll go all the way down
like lowriders, we'll fall as far back
as time goes by way of bone.

Oh, who cares if some of our teeth fall out?
We'll be like sharks and new sets will
push forward like fresh trays popping up in
cafeterias.

Then, we'll veer outside
to see what else we
can agitate and tumble up.

Our noses will combine with the universe.
Our noses will pulse with sensation.
Our noses will shimmy and revolve.

Then, when we're ready
after some barking and leaping
we'll lather up in a beach sand bath.
It will be like a YouTube recipe video.
we'll be marshmallows coated in graham crackers.

Before we go back inside,
we'll pant in gusts
and roll out our tongues

like red carpets.
No celebrities allowed—
only wind, only this whirling dust.

Paris

I had a horrible dream about you! You told me you were moving to Paris. That wasn't the horrible part though. The horrible part was that you were moving there exclusively to do heroin!

You weren't going to Paris to travel, or look at art, or teach, or to write, or study, or sit around eating delicious things made with large quantities of butter.

And worse, it sounded like you'd just lost any kind of connection to a meaningful life: interior or exterior. It was like the *you-ness* of you had disappeared. I was furious with you.

I shouted, "Heroin? Paris? What? Oh, you! How could you?" I yelled. I carried on and on. I paced around and waved my arms in a jazz of shock and dismay. I wept bitterly. I pounded the floor with my fists. "Why? Why?" I cried. You said "Oh come on, don't you think you're being a bit dramatic?"

You stood up then and opened a drawer on your nightstand. You pulled out a thick guide to doing heroin in Paris. You'd underlined various passages and had made multiple notes in the margins. On the inside front cover there was even a convenient pocket for needle storage.

I begged you to reconsider. You insisted that I had no idea what I was talking about. You said I was completely misinformed. You'd done research and I hadn't. "You know nothing about heroin in Paris," you said. "Nothing at all."

Then, in another part of the dream, I was somewhere else, maybe in Wisconsin or Iowa, somewhere in the Midwest, in someone's backyard, reading a postcard. It was from you, from Paris. Printed on one side was a scraggly drawing of a fountain. I turned the postcard over and you'd written something illegible about children, only you'd spelled *children, chilled wren* which made no sense at all. I called my friend M. about it and she said, "Classic addict behavior."

So, I have to make sure, you're not going to Paris are you? And if you are, it's not for shooting-up heroin reasons right? Because if you did do that, I would think about you and worry about you so much and I would curse that dumb heroin book and the dumbshit moron who wrote it and I'd curse the empty demon who built a nest in your brain to live inside of and ruin you. And if you never came back, eventually, I'd have to let you go, and letting go is the thing I'm the worst at.

Fortunes

You will work on an ecologically responsible cruise ship for 7 weeks, but your only job will be to count how many otters and whales you spot and then deliver the sum to the captain of the ship at dinner. Sometimes, at night, if you can't fall asleep, you will go up to the basketball court near the stern to shoot baskets under the moonlight. Everytime you make a basket you will sing a song that goes: *Made a basket, ketchup packet, in, in, in.*

You will notice when things in the world resemble belt loops. When you see these loops on fences, railings, underpasses, and bridges, you will weave belts through them and it will be like the whole world is your own potholder loom project from the 4th grade. You will loop and loop. The belts will be made of vines, string, thread, old dog leashes, jump ropes, and kite tails. You get the idea. You'll be so into it.

An extremely special baby will come to visit you and show you her fat tummy right away. She will point to her belly button and whisper, *yeah*. You will present her with a bowl of mint ice cream. You will feed her a bite and then you will pretend to take a bite, back and forth. She will demand the spoon, but will be delighted when you bring her the tiny Turkish teaspoon your friend Tina gave you when she moved to Arizona. And then this baby will proudly feed herself and shake her head yes, yes, yes, while her hair floats about her head in airy poofs. And when she's done eating, her face will have a glossy, patina—a wet, green-tinted, darlingdarling sheen.

Hot Potato

Wobbling, then settling
in her silver garment

complementing the fork
to the left of her

bouncing light off
a knife to her right

Self Portrait With Icicles

I've decided to cradle everything I can hold in my arms and so I do. You can see me cradling fruits, heaps of laundry, various books, the past, cans of beans and coconut milk, sponges, pouches of tomato soup and regret, seltzer: usually 2 bottles, one in each arm like twins.

I've come to see that cradling is a cutting edge technology because, think about it, to cradle something or someone is to turn part of oneself into a cradle and I believe if I'm lucky enough to come with this feature, I should make use of it.

So this is why, when I was walking home from the train on Wednesday and had already decided I wouldn't stop at the grocery store as I'd intended, but would instead, collect icicles in the grocery bag I had with me which was red by the way, like a mouth.

There were icicles hung in slick wet points and vines on the bicycle rack in front of the stairs and then on the iron fence surrounding the building on the corner and at the bottom of every sign too, and on the brick ledges and everywhere. They were blade-shaped windows, serious and opaque. Some were in groupings, flickering choruses, others were a long exhibit of hazy fangs. All of them were drippy wonderments, lacquered by design, as smooth as whales.

At home, I gathered them into a bouquet and gave it to myself as an award. An award for what? Maybe for being alive, or for being an icicle collector, perhaps for icicle appreciation? I wasn't sure. I wrapped the icicle bouquet in a blanket and cradled it. I took a photo of myself in the mirror for the ceremony.

Soon, I thought, these icicles will melt as they take their last baths in the water of themselves and disappear.

Dream Pool

In May, inside a dream
I found myself
married to Jerry Seinfeld

Everywhere we went people
would yell out,
Well, well, well if it isn't
Jerry and Barrie.
And they always
said his name first.

Later, Jerry was
showing me the indoor pool
he'd just installed.
We were looking at it
through such an odd little window

when all at once I remembered
those moments before you kissed me
when we were both 15.

You'd told me you were
a serious swimmer.

And as you were telling me
I saw a few wisps of your hair lift up
from the breeze of your voice.

I was so good, you'd gone on, so … fast
fast, like vroom, but with me, my own body,
not a car, and in water
before I…

You stopped.
I didn't need the details,
we were at the school
for big mistakes.
We were bad kids.
Everyone knew it.

It was then that you kissed me,
I'd been kissed just twice before
and I'd liked those two kisses alright
but the way *you* kissed me?

All at once, some kind of
pitcher appeared
in me and filled
all the way up.

You kidnapped our pain.
You revised it.

The Show

She said it was an excellent show and I should definitely watch it and so she would ask me from time to time if I'd watched it yet, and if I had, if I'd liked it and I'd say no, I haven't watched it yet, what is it called again, and she would tell me the name again and even text me the name as a reminder and then she'd talk at length about the latest episode of the show.

I enjoyed hearing about the episodes. The episodes had fully fleshed out characters with first and last names like Donovan Needle and Laila Harmonica, and the setting of the show sounded truly original because there was not only a ranch in it, but also a castle.

And what the characters said to each other when they wanted something and what they did to each other when they didn't get what they wanted, and what they were all dealing with felt so relevant, so current and the complications were so relatable and some of the unexpected shifts were what really got me and I found it all rather invigorating to hear about—like strong coffee.

And so it was always a little disappointing when in the midst of telling me about one of the episodes, after acting out the roles so believably, so perfectly, and captivatingly, even using various accents, even picking up whatever props happened to be around the house for demonstrating—a pot or a pillow—she'd stop and say, *I'm telling you too much. I'm ruining it. You just have to watch it.*

But I continued to forget the name of the show and the times I could recall the name, I'd also forget to watch it or I'd avoid watching it because maybe, I realized, I liked to watch what I wanted to watch on TV and use my eyes and attention for the gazing of my choosing and so I decided that the next time she mentioned it, I'd admit that I might never watch it and that I really might not even want to and so maybe she could simply continue to *be* the show *for* me. And I knew if I told her this, exactly what she'd say:

I can't believe you won't watch it, you really should watch it because even though you think I am giving it justice, I'm definitely not! I'm not TV! Okay? I'm not TV!

Will You Saunter

I want you to get me a thing that will be the right thing to handle this situation and then I want you to come here with the thing. But please don't just hand it to me and say, *Here, this will do the trick* because I won't know what to do with it. I don't even know what's wrong, just that something most certainly is and it has to do with me. I'd like you to ascertain what is wrong, exactly, and then apply the thing to the wrongness. I'm not asking you to be my doctor—more just someone who, knowing how I usually am, and how I could be again, knows what to do.

And honey, that is the reason why this is a love letter. The love part has to do with my confidence in you being the right woman to do this. You won't say, "Do it yourself. No one can fix anyone else." That's not what this is about.

You will understand that my allowing you to do it is doing it myself. I'll do this for you sometime, too, as soon as I can; I promise.

I'm sure that once you get whatever it is that you get, opening the package will be difficult because it will be complicated and unfair in multiple ways, but I just want you to prevail over the plastic, wire, and tape to get to the heart of the thing.

You can use tools to do this. I don't mind. You can even use knives. You are welcome to borrow tools from me. My tools are your tools in this love we share. So, yes, I'm giving you permission to wield tools. That should give you some indication of just how serious this is.

And once you open it, once you get past the packaging to the thing of it, even if you have to wrestle and wield all my knives, even if you swear in new and completely imaginative ways drawing upon all the reading you do, I still want you to be able to unfold and decipher the map-like instructions written in seventeen languages.

Please saunter around confidently and know what you're talking about. Even if it's just an act, try to make it a convincing act. Say, *Right, right we just need to put this here and this here and now hold on, hold on, just hold on.*

Okay? You don't need to act like any kind of stereotypical dude. No, just be grounded like someone who never misses yoga and listens to podcasts about emotional regulation and strategies for securing the future.

And then afterwards, please say, "There, it's done: Well now, that was easy. Look, that was all you needed. Everything is assembled and everything is in place. Everything is right again. Babe, you're good to go, now what would you like to do?"

And, it would be especially great, if when you say that last part, you could smile that way you do sometimes, when you have all kinds of loverish ideas up each one of your lacy & exceptional sleeves.

I'm Telling You

To get from point A to Point B, you have to dress up in yellow clothes including yellow socks and a yellow hat, and then you must put bands of black fabric on top of your yellow clothing so you resemble a bee, and then you should make a buzzing sound, but try not to go over the top with the buzzing.

Attempt a gentle buzzing; even a whispery kind of buzzing. Still, within these constraints, please buzz like you mean it and then make sure you have a hula hoop (either real or made up) and walk and hula hoop at the same time and then pretend you are swimming which is like air guitar, only with swimming, and then after you air swim, please air drum solo, and then air taco eat, and then air do something else because the last air activity is up to you, and then take a little nap, but no more than 17 minutes long, tops.

Then, open the fridge to scan the contents, but don't eat anything or throw anything away, just look, just stare, just take it all in. Take in the condiments in the door, the mustard and horseradish safe behind the sturdy, metal seatbelt. Take in the lone tortilla curling over its torn paper package and the plastic jug of water like an empty aquarium.

Finally, take a moment to grieve the broken ice maker which once had crushed ice or ice cubes and then remind yourself that ice cubes are only frozen water and you can make them anytime, anytime at all. Ice cubes are not out of reach for you. Ice cubes are achievable. They are no prize, no prize at all, but they aren't nothing either.

On Poetry

I'll begin with Carl Sandburg because a Sandburg is so much better than an iceberg, so much better, perhaps, than a Pittsburgh, but perhaps not? Pittsburgh has its charms. It is, as they say, a kind of Paris.

A Ginsburg is great too, but a Sandberg is the best kind of berg because of the sand and because of the *and* within the sand. The *and* makes the Sandburg a berg of joining and oh, how I love a unification berg! I do, I do. A unification berg is much better than a monotony berg. I've never met anyone who belongs to the fan club of a monotony berg.

Carl Sandburg said this about poetry: He said, "Poetry is the synthesis of hyacinths and biscuits."

Hyacinths come in multiple colors: Violet, orange, red, blue, pink, and the best hyacinths are robust with dense flower spikes. And what could be more exciting than dense flower spikes? Nothing, that's what.

Also, all hyacinths emerge from poisonous bulbs. Gloves are recommended.
Of course they are.
Gloves.

And now onto the biscuits. What kind of biscuits? Warm ones. Warm, fresh biscuits made with buttermilk, of course, and with butter too, slathered on lavishly, because why joke around with hybridity?

So, if Carl Sandburg is right, we're talking about poetry as something which could also be called a *biscisynth.*

How does this work exactly? Like this: The hyacinth speaks to the biscuit through the sound of the word *synthesis*. The synthesis is a tunnel, a portal, a transformation tube. Assonance is one of mating calls and so is alliteration. There are multiple calls made on multiple phones: Phonemes are the phones.

Also, roses.

Here's a parable on the matter
to take from what you will:

Once, my friend Chris went on a first date with someone he met through a dating site. They met at a crowded bar. The TVs were on in the bar and people were talking in a jumble and thumpy music was playing, too.

My friend Chris's date's name was Julietta. She said, "Let's get out of here." And he said "Okay, but where are we going?" And she said, "First on an errand, and then to my place."

The errand was to the corner store and Chris said Julietta bought something, but didn't want him to see what it was, so she asked him to close his eyes. She also shielded the thing she had, cupping it to her chest like a kitten.

"Did you peek?" I asked him.

"I did not," he told me. Then he said, "It may have been aspirin. It could have been condoms, tampons, chocolate or socks. I'll never know. It is all in the realm of the unknown."

And to that I say: What a realm the realm of the unknown is! So vast.

He told me he went with her to her apartment then. They walked there in the fall. The trees were changing their outfits in all the world's dressing rooms.

She asked him to sit once they got there and he did. She had a lime green couch. It was small, more like a loveseat than a couch, a velvet nest.

Then she said, "Listen Chris, I was hurt once, I was hurt badly, but I have invented a series of movements and when I do these extremely special, stylized movements I remain safe and I have chosen you to show them to, I have. Also, I have only revealed these gestures to one other person before, so this is really, really rare. Are you ready?"

He said, "I guess so."
She said, "I need you to *know* so."
"Ok," he said, "I know so."
"And then she did this… dance, this…"
"Show me," I said.
"I can't remember," he said.

"Was it poetic?" I asked.
"Not really," he said. "Well a little, a little in its fury."
"Oh. It had fury in it?"
"Yes, and it was choppy. It had a choppy, soft, eroticism with furious edges."
"Was it funny?" I asked.
"Not really," he said again. "Not to me, anyway. There was a lot of humanity in it and somehow it fed me and it seemed, I don't know… necessary. But the second it was over, I had to leave. I couldn't stay. And she knew I would leave, probably from looking at me, from looking at my face, my eyes, from not seeing something that she'd needed to see. She said, 'I shouldn't have chosen you; I chose wrong. Pretend you never saw this. Just go ahead and leave like leaves.'
"Can you believe she said that?" He said. "Leave like leaves?"
"Wow, so you left right then?" I asked.
"Yes," he said, "I left."

I looked at him then, and we sat with the biscisynth of all he'd told me, until it grew dark.

Down The Hill

One day we saw a hill and we decided to behold it and we saw that it was an exceptional hill so then we decided to roll down it and it was enjoyable to roll down because of the soft grasses being so accommodating and not scratchy at all

and the hill wasn't too steep either, so we decided to roll down it more often after we did it that first time, at least once a day, and that worked out for us quite nicely

and sometimes when we rolled down the hill we would say a word that came to mind, a word like *research* or *frequency* or *substantial* and sometimes we sang the words when we rolled and that was nice

and it was a little like how William Carlos Williams said *"When they give you lined paper, write the other way."*

because we felt we'd been given a hill and whereas most would walk down it or avoid it altogether, we'd decided on rolling, so that made us happy and made us rollmates beyond eating rolls and playing roles and that was terrific

and one day we woke up so early, so early, so early and went outside and there was all this dew on the grass, which covered the hill and it made the hill so wet and so full of gleam and the word that came to us that time turned out to be two words: *Anne Frank* (that was surprising!)

and so, as we rolled down the hill we said: Anne Frank, Anne Frank, and then we sung her name to the tune of *Row, Row Row Your Boat*

we sang:
Anne Frank, Anne Frank, Anne Frank
Anne Frank, Anne Frank, Anne Frank, Anne Frank
Anne Frank, Anne Frank, Anne Frank, Anne Frank, Anne Frank, Anne Frank, Anne Frank

and then, when we got to the bottom,
we were so very wet and being so, well, it felt like we *were* the hill and also like ourselves at the same time, and then it occurred to us how utterly vile it was that Anne Frank did not get to grow up and we knew that she should have been able to grow up so

that she could have written more than
a diary

and have had the chance to have a real adult
life and roll down a hill like the hill we had rolled down, a wet, dewy hill

and to have had a chance to sing her own
name to the tune of *Row Row Row Your Boat,*

but it also felt somehow, that we had
rolled *for* her, for Anne Frank, had rolled because she could not roll and so that was something new to do, to roll for others

and then we wrote this long sentence
because run-on sentences are better than their reputation would have everyone believe they are,

and also run-on sentences feel a lot like
rolling down a hill, only with words instead of with hills.

Liquidation

There was the business with the animals, the landlord, the broken machines, and the breakups. There was the business with the misunderstandings followed by the monumental sadness that was so heavy, we began calling it: *The Grand Piano.*

There was the business with the handshakes and the earthquakes and the fucked up lakes too and the pandemic and there was the business with the pajamas and the robes, the bathtubs, the toilets, the water in general, the rain, the rats, the plumbing and the pipes which also had to do with the original sadness, because there was all the crying that came with it.

Water with water.

This time came to be known as the *isness* of the business and the *isness* reverberated.

Its language was, *is, is, is, is, is.*

We couldn't get away from it. It was like a retractable leash that would no longer retract. It only extended and then extended some more.

But deep inside the business, there was a little laughter, but not much. It could only be located if we looked with fortitude and perseverance. We had to strive.

We needed to be spelunkers and spelunk inside the Great Cave of Sadness.

We needed equipment and headlamps to find any laughter at all during this total liquidation, during this time, when we were told, over and over and again and again, that everything must go.

Dream Job

My dream job, meaning the job I had in my dream was mostly sorting and I had to sort buttons and eggs and various hard candies and utensils like forks and chopsticks and there was another dream where my job was to sort too, but also count things, but I kept losing my place and had to start over right around 600 or 1010, and then there was another dream job where I was on the phone, but not speaking, just on it, waiting, like a phone meditation

and my favorite dream job was assembling mushrooms because in that dream, the mushrooms had various textures and sizes and colors and none of them were poisonous and my whole job was attaching the stems to the caps and it didn't matter if the correct stems went with the correct caps or not and so I found myself just trying out all kinds of intriguing mushroom combinations

and my boss at that job was myself because I asked the woman who seemed to be in charge if I was doing my job correctly and she said, *How am I supposed to know, you are the boss*, but when I woke up from that dream I realized that boss backward would be pronounced sob and I cried over that discovery because it seemed important and so, at that moment, my job in real life was to be a crying person who had mushroom assembling dreams

and I hoped that in my next dream I had a job that was just as wonderful and I hoped it had something to do with waves and flowers, maybe assigning flower types to waves and maybe I could be in some kind of extremely tall lifeguard chair and as the waves came in I'd have a megaphone and shout, *Here comes Rhododendron, here comes Begonia, here comes Rose, here comes Daffodil,* and I think if I don't ever dream that dream, I will just give myself that job in real life and when I do will be so satisfied that if I took a job satisfaction survey, my job satisfaction would be off the charts

Transfer

The other day I was driving down Ashland Avenue and when I was stopped at the red light near Wilson, I saw someone who looked almost exactly like someone I'd known years before, only the person I'd known years before had been such an unhappy sort of person, a person who never seemed to get what she most wanted, which was probably just a regular kind of life with a little extra, like maybe not only an affordable place to live, but a place close to the train because she'd never learned to drive and hadn't ever been interested in learning.

But the person I was seeing, who I believed was the same person I'd once known, was not sad at all, not even a little, and that is really something in these times. Also, she was kissing another woman and was being kissed back and they were both grinning inside the kissing. I could see it.

But then, I realized that the woman kissing and being kissed and now hugging and now laughing and now crossing the street with the other woman holding hands and swinging them like a letter M shaped swing, could not possibly be the woman I'd known years before, because she'd have grown older, just as I had. Once you're over 50, you don't look 30. That's just how being a person works.

I do need to tell you that even though she wasn't the person I'd known, I imagined somehow that the combination of me thinking of her while also seeing someone who so closely resembled her that perhaps some joy had been transferred to her wherever she was and that some rapture found her and shook her.

3

Ripple

The greasy teen at the petstore
(nametag: Don) suggested
I float a lettuce leaf
on top of the water
to draw out
the mystery snails
from the shadowy corners of
my aquarium

But Don failed to mention
the happiest, fattest guppy of them all

the one

with the swishing, flicking,
onyx-studded, dazzlingdazzling, dotted tail, the
one I'd named Stunner would

select that green-spined leaf of romaine with ruffled edges
as a bed to die on

How Things Are

In our past lives, my friends and I were deeply fulfilled and we took care of things and we were successful and diligent and we were industrious and methodical and balanced, and tender too, so tender. But in this life we are depressed and so we try new regimens or give up on the regimens we'd planned on beginning, but have not yet begun, especially those involving exercise and organization and we do not make the calls we need to make or measure up to the standards of the parents we had wanted to be and sometimes we eat candy for breakfast or let our kids eat candy for breakfast or only maple syrup without pancakes in little paper cups and the TV is on quite a bit and also has a presence, a fleshiness too, almost like an additional family member and sometimes in this life we just hand our children our phones, we just let our children go wild with our phones and sometimes we do not get our phones back for many hours, but in our past lives we'd get them back, we would, we definitely would.

And it's sad that this life feels like a flop especially because sometimes it's just too difficult to remember to put the wash in the dryer until the next day when the wet clothes have already begun to smell of mildew and of cat pee too even though there is not a cat, because some or all of the family members are allergic to cats, so who knows why the cat pee smell and Jesus Christ this life feels like a constant starting over, like a constant begging to have another chance and then getting one, getting another chance, even four or five or six chances, but then failing again and ending up one day on a rare afternoon when no one else is home with some pot someone gave us maybe two years ago that we had kept in an envelope behind the cleaning supplies and sometimes in this life we end up smoking it in the bathroom, standing in the bathtub with the door locked exhaling out the window with a giant mixing bowl of Raisin Bran and a soup ladle for a spoon and some legitimate awe at this particular life and just how it's all turned out so far.

Jessica

That July, when I turned six
I was given a magic set
The only trick I liked
was the quarter disappearer:
a rectangular, black
piece of plastic with a
secret compartment

I'd perform the trick over and over
for my neighbor Jessica Grabowski

What a beautiful child
was the thing people were always
saying about Jessica
I wanted to impress her

As for me: I had a lumpy tangle in the back of my head that
I wouldn't let anyone get to
I had sticky popsicle juice on my
face, and mosquito bites I couldn't leave alone
I still sucked my thumb
I was afraid of most people

Also, I was trying to count to a million
I had a notebook of hash marks to keep track
Jessica thought this in particular was
the stupidest thing she'd ever heard of
I never told her my first idea had been to try for infinity

For the trick, I'd press the sides of the box and
a tray with an eye-sized window would appear
I'd place a quarter into it and slide it shut
Jessica would roll her eyes with the skill of a teenager

Abracadabra, I'd shout
I'd slide out the tray and
voila, the quarter had disappeared
Fanfare was everything

I was the only kid who loved the
required orange safety flag
on the back of my bike.
I rang and rang the handlebar bell
I had a silver squeeze-horn, too
My Dad said the only thing
missing was a monkey

After I'd been Jessica's personal magician
for awhile, I'd say:

Isn't it cool? Isn't it so cool?
The quarter hides where we can't see it
It has its own apartment
It could be watching TV

Jessica said, *That's nuts.*

No, I said, This trick is like your hideaway
sofa, my sister's trundle bed, a hermit crab
Don't you get it?

I have always wanted to be visible
and invisible
to be in the world
but also alone in the dark
counting into the
mystery of infinity.

I Knew the Other Ways It Could Be

I was on a plane once so long ago, and the woman sitting next to me had never been on a plane before.

She was young, perhaps nineteen or so, and she explained that she was travelling to visit her boyfriend who was a Freshman at college in Atlanta and that he would be meeting her at the gate.

This was at a time when you could still meet people at the gate and see all the sweet reunions, which are not as common to see now, in the baggage claim area. A gate is so immediate and so much time has passed that by the time you get to the baggage claim area, well, it is just not the same. Of course, it's not.

The young woman liked the plane ride a great deal and was so happy about seeing the clouds right next to her like floating travel companions, and she was so enchanted by the sliding window shade and the sturdy thick glass window and the view of big things made tiny from such an astonishing height.

And the inside of the plane delighted her, too. She loved the tray tables and the controls, all the buttons overhead. She especially enjoyed fiddling with the air control's suck and whoosh.

She appreciated everything about the ride including her complimentary beverage and her complimentary meal and the way it fit on the tray table so exactly. She could hardly understand the people reading books or magazines on the plane when there was so much excitement to experience already.

She said, "I've been looking forward to this for such a long time. I just think this is amazing. We really are flying. We really are in this gigantic thing that is like a bird with wings, only it's not a bird. Everything about this is an invention!"

Her enthusiasm put some magic and dimension back into what had become familiar to me.

Then we landed which was of course a wonder to her too, especially the thump at the end. We said goodbye and she gathered up her things. She had a small backpack decorated with patches and pins. One of the pins said, *Go For It!*

I was right behind her as we made our way through the narrow aisle. When we emerged, I saw which waiting boy was the one that she called *boyfriend* right away.

He had blond hair and was plump in a sensuous way, like a pie. He was pink in the face from the blood in him rushing up so suddenly at the sight of her. He took his hands out of his pockets and lifted them up in a spontaneous gesture that welcomed and reached out all at once. He seemed to vibrate a bit too and had to steady himself as if from a jolt.

He was bashful and his bangs obscured some of his expressions, but the feeling inside him was not bashful at all. It was a sprawling kind of feeling and it glowed out from him as she walked directly into its scope.

It was so dazzling how she did that even though she did it so naturally, as if she did not know a different way it could be, the way the whole thing could be, as I certainly did know, oh I did, and at the time, I was only a few years older than she was.

So I gathered all I could from those lovers and stored it away for so many years. I didn't take it out much to study at all.

But now, I'm giving it away like an heirloom. I'm passing it on. It has no chips or cracks. So, here, take it.

Breakfast

What is beauty anyway?
Not a doily or a sunset,
not a baby, dimpled,
wearing a sunhat,
swinging on a swing
in the park, near the river.

Not a guitar
with its dark portal
into everywhere.

Not even the antique haiku
about the wet duck
catching a smolt.

Beauty is sneakier than all that.
She's nothing at all like pretty.

She catches you off guard
like someone stepping on your foot accidentally
on the subway.

Beauty is a stun gun, an unlikely detour from
the rural reality you knew just
a moment ago.

You can call out, *Beauty, oh Beauty, where are you? Show yourself to me.*

All Beauty hears is *blah, blah, blah*
Like so many Charlie Brown adults.

She will however, respond to a true demand-
a gigantic longing, an offering of emptiness.

Pockets turned all the way over
into dusty white peaks, yourself emptied
from yourself.
Beauty likes to wait until you give up.

Take this morning
a mess on the counter:
instant coffee powder spilled in tiny heaps,
an open carton of milk,
a dirty cup, a triptych of shiny
marmalade globs

And then all at once,
light embossed the room
as a great triangle of birds flew
inside every corner of my eye.

Celebrate Shmelabrate

I refuse to celebrate the glistening spider's web or even the thread-expelling, net-maker herself.
Both of them can go to hell.

So can the three sunflower petals that have corkscrewed their way onto the web & are now perfectly adhered to it. Yeah, yeah, it's a masterpiece.
Who cares?

Oh, and it figures that the petals would be in haiku formation vibrating gently among the tiny, lacquered contact lenses of dawn, also known as dewdrops.
Whatever.

Angelwatching

Many are rather childlike.
A few seem to be obsessed with the Italian Renaissance.
Some are perpetually nude and unabashedly so.
Most have wings, but over 40 percent never fly.

I believe that the wings are mostly for show so that angels can be recognized as angels.
If angels want to be incognito (as in fly under the radar)
they fold up their wings and behave nonchalantly as if they have no wings at all.

Squirrels behave similarly with acorns. When other squirrels are around, they hoard and bury them, then act as if they've never heard of an acorn in their entire squirrel lives.

Many angels are familiar with both the tooth fairy and Santa Claus, but they are not believers in either. Angels are hypocritical as they have no problem believing in the existence of themselves.

Some angels are quite fat, and they delight in being so, as fat is considered a great boon among angels. Angels hope for fat a lot.

Angel's fashion sense isn't much. They are only partly responsible for this as the garments available to angels are rather limited.

I've heard angel garments are procured in places similar to places where uniforms are sold to people and also, that the golden waist ropes are hard to come by. It may be the same when it comes to chains and ghosts. I'll try to find out.

Most of the garments angels wear, as you may have seen in various illustrations and paintings, are rather billowy.

Some angels even look as if they are wearing draperies and that is rather unfortunate.
But let us not forget that some angels have halos and that is so fortunate.

Angels don't use computers or cell phones, but they do occasionally wish they could use these things. Angels have their own technology. How this technology works is all very hush, hush.

Angels like to watch their own form of TV and they are always so vague about it. It's difficult to know what it is exactly. It may consist of watching rainbows along with other forms of light. But if that is the case, why would they call it TV?

It's possible that angel TV is simply the act of watching people. They watch us wash dishes and send emails. They watch us cry and grieve and die.

Perhaps they should call it theater instead.

Angels come in a variety of ages, and tend to stay the same ages for years and years.

Angels and clouds get along quite well.
Angels and the moon get along quite well too.
Angels have a fairly good relationship with the sky at large.

Some angels are translucent, and some only appear to be translucent. With some angels the translucency is an optical illusion, but such a convincing one!

Angels love to halve clouds with special cloud knives. They are given these knives at some point by the head angel, who resides within each angel's particular district.

Sometimes angels pretend clouds are loaves of bread and construct cloud sandwiches.

Angels and ghosts have a lot in common. The only difference between them is that angels help people and as a general rule, ghosts prefer haunting instead.

Angels do make mistakes, all kinds of mistakes
but one thing they do not do is make out.

Angels do not have a sexuality but they are
fascinated by the concept of love.

Angels definitely do not have arrows, cupid included.

The whole arrow thing was a misunderstanding
which may have stemmed from the sparrows.

See, angels keep sparrows as pets.
The sparrows can be found perching on the tips of their wings.

Wings on wings is the name of the game, my friend—
wings on wings.

What is particularly arresting is when angels with
sparrows perched upon their wings fly over snow
in the late morning hours
because if you are lucky you may
see their adorable double shadows
upon what is known by the angels
as the canvas of the world.

Unwelcome

I had a fling with morning
until afternoon pushed her pawn
Then day's balloons descended
dappling the lawn

And later still, with fate of day
long ago decided,
I had no choice
night's guests came in—
insisting they'd been invited

Parade of One

When the world is a lackluster,
lopsided pageant when it is unruly
and violently jabs in all directions
when the tubas keep their starched fists
permanently closed and the French horns have
never had any butter.

Why not look up to the planetary parade instead?
When all the planets float themselves
over to 17 across in order
to occupy their spots
on the invisible crossword of night.

Or, perhaps admire the pageant of
celery stalks wrapped
in their tattered
green scarves as they are
misted in the Co-op

Failing that, consider a parade of one
like the young woman I read about
who was walking on Millerton Road, near
Millerton lake, in California.

She was naked, with wet hair,
a faint mustache,
nothing more.

No, celery
No towel
No baton
No snare

When the police came with sirenblare,
careening out to greet her
she told them she'd been swimming in
the lake because she was in fact, a mermaid.

Still shivering, teeth chattering, she led their gaze
down to her feet, to her webbed toes in particular,
to the extraordinary hammocks of skin between each one
and smiled.

Counting

When you are counting, whatever it is you are counting: coins, buttons, ballots, cookies, the remaining minutes, seconds, hours, all the cars until the bus comes, your age, how many days until later, the number of rusty-edged, pink quincinera skirts falling from the magnolia tree and gathering into a godpile at the base of the trunk.

When you are counting your own teeth, stripes on a striped something—a zebra, a barcode, a pin-striped suit, overalls. a bedspread, wallpaper, a tiger.

When you are counting, count me in.
When you are including, include me.

If something repeats, if something is arranged in a repeating pattern, a sequence—if it repeats again and again and again, count me in.

Put me in there, so I'll be there
along with everything else.

Let's Argue for Pretending in a Pretend Court

You pretend to be a judge. Your gavel is a spoon, a chopstick, maybe a pen

It doesn't matter if you bang it on the dresser, the table, the floor, the wall

It doesn't matter.

Just bang.

We'll prove that elephants can be here just with the mention of them and then, boom, here they are.

Boom.

The elephants braid their trunks, their ears a series of grey crepes, flapping in pans of air.

Next case: We must prove ice creams too, ice creams of many flavors and varieties, yes coconut, yes chocolate, and even one with a raspberry creek snaking through a snowy, vanilla landscape. Here they are.

Mentioning brings things into a field.
This is our summation.

Our final argument?

Well, your honor and members of the jury, you must admit that infants and cellos can arrive via mentioning them too. All at once, here they are, together.

Boom, again,

Oh, just look at the infants gurgle and stretch out their masterfully sectioned arms. And I know you can't help but marvel at all those gleaming, caramelized cellos.

The Cardboard Piano

I'd inherited a piano from my Grandpa.
No one else in the family wanted it.
It was an upright, with various
marks and indentations on its skin,
its wood that is-itself.

I thought maybe the piano had
grown bored in the basement
where it had been living in
solitary confinement, unplayed
for years. Maybe the piano had
managed to find a sharp nail to
gouge with, along with some hands.

My husband and I set about
hiring piano movers.This was before
the divorce. My God,
the kids were still babies.

The staircase to our floor
was steep and narrow.
People were always hitting
their heads on the ceiling.
It was single file only
never two at a time.

The piano movers told us they weren't optimistic
about making it work, so they'd have to practice first,
using a cardboard piano they'd cut to
the exact measurements of the regular piano.

It would be like a dress pattern.
It would be like a dress rehearsal, too.

And when they brought over the cardboard
piano, I almost applauded. What a rare
same-size shadow kind of art thing.

It had scratchy music too
like a push broom sweeping a sidewalk
like squirrels on a roof, all pitterpatter and hurry.

It was a sandpaper, treebark,
pingpong, sawdust quartet.

I loved how the piano movers
worked out just how it would go up
the stairs, turn at the corners,
and make it over to the spot we'd chosen.

The movers pretended the cardboard
piano was heavy—for practice but still
they whispered, not a yell, not one grunt.

The next week, when they came back
with the real piano, I took the kids
to the park straight away.
I knew heavy was heavy.

We didn't need to see the real struggle up—
the heaving, the bearing of so
much weight.

There would be enough struggling later,
for all of us.

Son: Age Three

I walking.
I seeing so many tings when I walking.
I see dis tree.
I walking more.
I hungy now and I eat dis.
I eat dis nice thing.
Dis called orange.
I need anoner piece.
We share dis orange gether.
Now I take off shoes.
Now I put on shoes. Easy.
I zip dis zipper.
You start it.
I zip the rest.
It goes zzzzz. See?
I gonna walk again now.
I gonna go to a park with us.
I gonna slide down the slide
I gonna swing on da swing.
You push.
I gonna do a jump trick.
Look.
I gonna pick up this ting.
This ting is a rock.
It's hebby.
I put it down.
There you go rock.
Can we stay more whiles?
Look a bug. It walking too. Hi bug.
Where it Mom go?
It hab a Mom like me?
This odder ting is a grass piece.
I pulled it.
The color is green.
This is a leaf.
I hold it.
It green too.
Most things are green Mama.

Green and blue too and
odder ones.
Everting wit colors.

Because I Still Believe in Romance

I want to date a vending machine with good snacks in it-good, rare snacks like a baked potato in a tinfoil bodysuit or peanut-butter toast with a honeydrizzle signature.

I want to date a carwash tree which some still call by their former name: *weeping willow*, but that only made sense during those years when the carwash trees were grief-stricken. They are doing so much better these days, hence the change.

I want to date a playground with a rhythmic, creaky swing set, a red and white striped corkscrew slide, and wooden benches replete with mushroom birthing centers beneath them.

I want to date a wave with a foamy mustache/ beard combination and wet, green wings that fan out and out, turn over, gather blue, and repeat forever.

Check it Out

The beach is a library and you can just check everything out and you can check it all the way out with your eyes and your ears and your hands and feet and your nose or you can go shopping at the beach with no money or with pretend shell money and you can buy some waves with your shell money and a sky line of sky and a water line of water and you can buy so much seaweed arranged in decadent clumps on the sand and also spiraling about in the water like crocheted shawls and green witch wigs.

And if you wait long enough, you can have a moon, too, and when it is full, see the great rippled beam it casts with its built-in flashlight upon the lake. And if you cannot wait until night, no problem; you can still have a horizon line in daylight, and the horizon line is the seam of the world.

And you can check out the book of seagulls and geese and pigeons and ducks and wind and you can check out the whole beach and keep it for as long as you like without overdue fines or a need to return any of it. It's already you. You are already it.

Crosswalk

What if the three lights on traffic signals correspond to mind, body, and spirit?

If this is the case, then green corresponds to the body because the body is just like tall grasses, algae floating on a pond, dense forest mud, and mosses, too.

Also, green carries the meaning of go within its illuminated circle and the body goes and moves too and trees are green bodies. Grasshoppers have green blood. We are alive. Look, a frog. Go to it. Aliveness takes green breaths drawn from a green core.

And surely, yellow corresponds to spirit, so as to suggest light emanating from the sun. Also, caution too, when going out into the sun: Proceed carefully. Apply lotion. Slow down.

I would argue that the yellow circles are, in fact, small suns only without sets and rises unless you count their beams appearing and disappearing, as sets and rises, which I do. Of course, I do.

Red corresponds to the mind. Red and mind both end with a "d" as does "end." Make no mistake, these are meaningful pointers. As minds wander, red demands attention. The red circle tells you, you must stop, but also that it is a round book with just one, glowing page describing with precision, a red cardinal circumnavigating a newly painted red bench in Autumn.

Beloved

I seem to possess an unreasonable feeling of personal gladness about your existence. It's similar to the way I've felt about kitchen matches, the wooden ones that come in a cardboard box and open like a drawer. Kitchen matches thrill me because they are more or less a fire-kit inside a coffin. And just how many coffins have striking panels on both sides? An argument could be made that all matches are humble spectacles, even the flimsy ones that come in books are books of fire.

I have also at times had to restrain myself from tasting paint-chips at the hardware store because the names of the colors call out so loudly to me: Urban Lime, Thunderdawn, Wet Grove, Smoky Pashmina, Hushed Peach.

But that is beside the point.

The point is, that if I even remotely liked the expression, *You pull at my heart strings* that is what I would say to you, but I have never liked the idea of strings attached to anyone's heart, as if the heart were a marionette or worse, a tampon. I like to imagine hearts without strings.

I do, however, think it is lovely that hearts have chambers like bed and breakfasts in England. I've never been to England, so I don't really know what I'm talking about, but you do occupy some little part of my heart, some room. You don't live there of course, but still, my feeling for you has redecorated a little alcove and I sense an improvement; as if someone had come inside and made up the bed and swept up the dust bunnies out from all the corners.

In any case, what I'm trying to tell you and what I should have said at the beginning of this letter is that I spent some time, some hours really, making you a Wikipedia page—I listed your accomplishments and some of your most appealing features.

I left out any unfortunate details because no matter what anyone says, I still believe there is such a thing as privacy. Since you don't have a name, I simply listed you as *Beloved*. Unfortunately, either the people or the algorithm at Wikipedia decided you weren't famous enough to have a Wikipedia page and so the entry was removed. I received an email from them, which I answered, of course, but it was returned as undeliverable.

In my response, I'd tried to clarify that I was not in any way writing about Toni Morrison's masterful novel which coincidentally shares your name: *Beloved*. I wrote that I was indeed aware that there already were pages for both Toni Morrison and *Beloved* the book. Also, I wasn't trying to make light of the information superhighway or abuse wikis or pedias of any kind. I tried to explain that I just wanted you to be googleable so that you would come up, as you should come up; like a flower or a vine, an elevator, a ladder, a staircase, the sun, the moon, a subject. I wanted you to come up like any one of those things, any one of those things at all.

Enchantments

There enchanting objects and this is true regardless of all the so much less than enchanting things which abound in contemporary life and sometimes recognizing the enchantment of these objects can create a feeling (however, unrealistic, however fleeting) of enchantment because there are pens that not only write with the ink inside them—and ink of course is the blood of pens, but which also light up on the other end, so that the owner of the pen may write in the dark, on a train, or in a small corner of a dark bedroom late at night where loved ones are sleeping nearby.

And speaking of things that light up, and which also happen to be objects of enchantment—there are tiny, tiny chandeliers meant for doll houses, but there is no rule that anyone has to have a dollhouse in order to have a light like this and so anybody could just procure a tiny dollhouse chandelier and keep it with them in case they are in need of a bit of enchantment, which really, when you consider the state of affairs, who isn't in need of enchantment, just who isn't?

Also, think of wristwatches, which are, in reality, tiny clocks that wrap around wrists like wrist-belts and consider how enchanting it might be to have a wrist belt and a waist belt that match exactly and the idea of something like a matching watch and waist belt set is so enchanting that to even to think of such things is an enchanting activity on its own.

And, what about the nests secured within the limbpits of many trees as well as the branches they balance on, and the nooks they fit it into. Nests are utilitarian sculptures made by bird mothers who don't even have arms with which to carry all of the supplies necessary to create them. Enchanting.

And many nests have eggs in them which will break open at some point to reveal birds with damp newly sprouted feathers which are the body flowers of birds and if that is not enchanting, I don't know what is, except of course the delicate work of the spider who has been been crocheting something she calls her *Festival of Rectangles* for hours between the spokes of a bicycle wheel propped up near the graffitied, metal bench.

Hot Flash

I was building castles in my hair
I made the windows out of
of contact lenses.

There were toothpick drawbridges.
They poked me in the night, giving
me acupuncture.

I wore amber beach glass sunglasses—
they made everything turn Coca Cola,
bubbled and brown.

I know now that whatever wrinkles water,
also wrinkles me

we compared our rippled necks
looking for similarities.

Unhook, unhook me! I yelled to the
whatever and waited for a bra undone
sensation.

When it came, it was subtler
than I'd imagined, but I could still feel it

I found a working lighter in the sand.
I lit it, pressing the silver gear
to the tongue.

I set the flame to the highest setting,
a hot, hot flash.

O menopause, you are the
comma I get to keep.

Arrangement

Here, I've brought you some imaginary flowers
Mostly gladiolas and roses, one dahlia, a
smattering of forget-me-nots throughout

No vase or water required

You are welcome to give them away
I have plenty, a garden's worth, more
You do too

Barrie Cole is a critically acclaimed Chicago-based writer who has written more than 15 plays including *Reality is an Activity, Capacity, Meaning is Tricky, Reverse Gossip, Elevator Tours and Fruit Tree Backpack* along with numerous poems, essays, monologues, alphabet works and hybrid works many of which have been read and performed in shows and venues like Story Sessions, Write Club, Kore' Press's Motherfield, The Poetry Foundation, Based on a True Story, City Winery, Essay Fiesta, The Neo Futurarium, The Steppenwolf Garage, and others. Her plays have been produced by multiple companies including Theater Oobleck, Curious Theatre Branch, The Prop Theatre, Sweetback, and Labyrinth Arts. Her work has received multiple Critic's Choice selections and has been published in various magazines and anthologies including *Windy City Queer. Chicago Stories, Half and One, The Twin Bill and others.* Poet Alison Luterman says, "To enter the pages of *Lacquer is a Thrilling Word* is to walk inside the wild and wonderful, kaleidoscopically shape-shifting mind of Barrie Cole, appreciating an odd truth bomb here, a moment of delight or humor there, and now and again a totally unexpected light ray of divine wisdom shooting through a dusty stained-glass window that was somehow exported from an ancient Gothic cathedral to a grocery store in downtown Chicago. There are too many delightful lines to quote in a blurb, but let's just say that she had me at 'I am still a good person if I have had an unfortunate haircut, the kind where there are bangs of insanity, the kind wherein cutting more could not even begin to improve it, a haircut that makes purchasing a wig a genuine consideration and I am still a good person if I paid the bill late and I was too anxious to attend the party and too anxious to say hello to the neighbor and so pretended not to see her at all and this was no surprise, because I do this more often than I do not, but I am still good. Probably.' I'll leave you to discover the rest on your own."

www.ingramcontent.com/pod-product-compliance
Lightning Source LLC
LaVergne TN
LVHW090533110826
845146LV00003B/1078

* 9 7 9 8 8 9 9 9 0 4 6 9 1 *